BEST DEFENSE

Countering Crime and Terrorism When Traveling

by
Norman Rheault

Llumina Press

ISBN: 1-59526-248-2
Printed in the United States of America by Llumina Press

Library of Congress Cataloging-in-Publication Data

Rheault, Norman.
  Best defense : Countering crime and
terrorism when traveling / by Norman Rheault.
      p. cm.
  Includes bibliographical references (p.   ).
  ISBN 1-59526-248-2 (pbk. : alk. paper)
  1. Travel--Safety measures. I. Title.
G151.R45 2004
613.6'6'08891--dc22

                                        2004012768

To
Diane

ACKNOWLEDGEMENTS

I wish to thank especially Kathryn Agnes McMahon
and Bill Robertson

ABOUT THE AUTHOR

As former head of security in Canada for a U.S. aircraft manufacturer with defense contracts, Norman Rheault received specialized training in countering crime and terrorism which he used to brief his company's executives when traveling in high risk countries.

In 1995, he developed as a management consultant, a training tool on the subject of air travel safety which was published in North America.

Norman Rheault has worked in overseas countries and he is an experienced traveler. In addition to his management practice, he gives seminars to corporations who have executives traveling in high-risk environments.

SPECIAL NOTE TO THE READER

We have gone to great lengths to provide current information with regard to aviation regulations and travel legislation. However, with the constant changes in the travel industry, it is wise to consult the numerous web sites at the end of this book to ensure up-to-date information. You will also find many ways and methods that can protect you from criminal aggressions. Be advised that the author cannot be held accountable for any outcome since each person is unique and may react differently to a given set of circumstances.

We welcome your contribution for future editions by sharing with us books, websites or other safety tips. We will make it a point to notify you by e-mail of the next editions. You may contact us at:

safertrip101@yahoo.com

CONTENTS

BEST DEFENSE

INTRODUCTION

Anyone who has traveled by plane since September 11, 2001 has had apprehensions about being a victim of terrorism.

Although the risks have been reduced, U.S. authorities have said on many occasions: **"It's not a question of if we have another terrorist incident, it's a matter of when"**.

To make matters more worrisome, Al-Qaeda is not the only active terrorist organization, although they are the most visible in the media for reasons we all know. The Terrorism Research Center (an independent institute) identifies a list of 159 terrorist organizations active in 2003 around the world. Together, they have perpetrated 1,355 terrorist attacks in 2003 resulting in 1,321 fatalities and 2,949 injuries. A short list of these countries includes: Russia, France, Spain, Mexico, Italy, Thailand, Nepal, Morocco, Turkey, Saudi Arabia, Indonesia and India.

Innocent people were killed in hotels, restaurants and streets although our major concern remains being caught in a plane being used as a guided missile. Now that security has been tightened to access the aircraft, the next attacks may be of a different nature. The risk level that used to characterize only a few countries in the 1980s has now migrated to the rest of the world. Who would have thought that the peaceful island of Bali would be the scene of a brutal bombing in a nightclub, killing hundreds of innocent tourists in October 2002? We now know that the threat has been extended to countries involved in the Afghanistan and Iraq wars.

Crime and terrorism can happen at any time, even when you are not traveling, but if you apply the measures provided in this guide and you adopt the proper safety behavior, you will make yourself significantly less vulnerable.

We have extensively researched the best advice from security professionals, Federal Aviation Agency publications, retired Special Forces and confidential counter-terrorism documents given to U.S. military personnel traveling abroad. Once you read this booklet, you will want to keep it as a valuable reference checklist.

Please take the time to read it all; it will make your future trips less worrisome and you will still continue to enjoy traveling. Our wish is that you or your family return safely from all your future journeys!

GOLDEN RULES OF BEHAVIOR

Awareness, alertness and discretion

Your ability to avoid trouble depends greatly on a calm but sustained vigilance. Is there anything out of place in your surroundings? You will see later on in this guide what to look for in an airport; on the streets of a foreign country, and in and around your hotel. Be alert to suspicious individuals. You will learn how to recognize ploys used by pickpockets and even a ritual used by suicide bombers moments before they detonate their explosives.

Always use covered nametags for your luggage. Anyone can read your address when waiting in line to check in at the airline counter. You don't want to come home to an empty house. Put your address at work for additional protection.

Be extremely careful about giving personal information to strangers during your trip. Casual talk in the hotel lobby about your whereabouts for the day can signal to the wrong people when your room is free for a visit. We will give you numerous tips to protect your room from unwanted visits.

Changing your behavior will do more for your safety than any protective apparel.

Keep a low profile

Your best bet is to remain invisible, and since that's impossible, at the present moment, your behavior, dress and mannerisms should remain unnoticed. You need to blend in as much as possible with the local people. Do not advertise who you are and where you come from and avoid hanging around in large groups. Although you may be tempted by curiosity, keep away from any demonstrations and civil disturbances; you could be thrown in jail just because you happen to be there.

BEFORE DEPARTING:
WHAT YOU NEED TO KNOW

What you need to know about your destination can make the difference between a great trip and a nightmare. Know your destination, or expect the unexpected.

The world's political climate is changing on a daily basis and not always for the better. Rising violence is emerging in what used to be "tourists' sanctuaries". Whether you travel for business or pleasure, you need to get information about the country you are visiting with regard to the people, culture, religion, local customs along with local health restrictions, when applicable (i.e.: epidem-

> *Dress to blend in with the average native. Nobody needs to know you are a foreigner.*

ics). Traveling without this knowledge is a serious mistake.

How to find what you are looking for:

In addition to the sources quoted in this guide, you can search the web for newsgroups, forums and bulletin boards relevant to your destination. Don't get all your information from tourists' sites; try to contact travelers who have already been there to get a more impartial opinion.

Just as an example, did you know that:

- In certain Muslim countries, you could go to jail for possession of alcohol or erotic literature.

- Certain narcotics and amphetamines are prohibited in Middle-Eastern countries, even if your doctor prescribes them.

- In many Asian countries, you can be fined for spitting or throwing a cigarette butt on the street.

Never make jokes about having a bomb or a firearm in your possession; airport personnel are trained to react when they hear these words. Penalties are severe and can include time in prison. A Canadian cabinet minister had to resign for making such a statement while passing security.

Until very recently, you were not allowed to chew gum in a public place in Singapore.

- In many countries with military dictatorships, you can create serious legal problems for yourself if you take pictures of government buildings or military guards.

In the past, countries used to be categorized by three levels of threats: low, medium and high risk; but since September 11, 2001, the above categories no longer apply. The terrorists' playing field has spread to the whole planet!

Although the media attention focuses mainly on casualties in the Middle East / Persian Gulf region, the last six years of available data up to the end of 2003 show startling statistics. Western Europe leads the world in the number of domestic incidents for that period with 2,086 cases. The following chart also shows that the South Asia region ranks third in domestic and overall incidents.

Terrorist Incidents By Region
From 12/26/1997 To 11/19/2003

Total Incidents: 9024   **Total Fatalities: 11810**   **Total Injuries: 24343**

Region	International	Domestic	Total
North America	4	87	91
Western Europe	205	2086	2291
Eastern Europe	62	771	833
Latin America	86	1238	1324
East & Central Asia	13	44	57
South Asia	83	1423	1506
Southeast Asia & Oceania	44	305	349
Middle East/Persian Gulf	453	1855	2308
Africa	78	187	265

Note: Data updated on November 24, 2003.

Source: RAND-MIPT terrorism incident database

Today, the political climate and the potential for terrorist attacks makes the risks level as whimsical as the weather. Fresh information on the country's security status is imperative, and you will see later on in this chapter how to find it.

In addition to individual country threat assessment, the United States Department of Homeland Security issues on a permanent basis the risk level on American soil which should be a good indicator of precautions to take even when going abroad. The threat scale is as follows:

CODE	RISK LEVEL
RED Severe	Severe
ORANGE High	High
YELLOW Elevated	Significant
BLUE Guarded	General Risk
GREEN Low	Low Risk

The threat level is determined by multiple sources, but mainly by CIA field agents and decoded Internet traffic transmissions. Those threats are to be taken seriously when you travel, regardless of your means of transport.

What information should you seek and where to get it?

First of all, you should clear the basic stuff with your travel agency. They can supply you with information on the following subjects:

- visa requirements

- local currency

- luggage allowances

- vaccination requirements

- which calling cards to use

- passport requirements for children

- basic local customs.

If you are meeting people in the visited country, ask them for a list of "do's and don'ts". If you are going to a country that you know will be different politically and culturally from anything you have seen before, you should contact the local consulate of the visited country. We will tell you later what information to ask for. You can also contact your embassy in the visited country to get their point of view on any precautions you should take before leaving.

If you wish to save time, here is the most comprehensive site to collect pertinent information on any country in the world. The U.S. Department of State updates a web site every day in its section of "The Bureau of Consular Affairs". You will find everything you need to know and more. Here is a list of topics you will find for the country you are doing the research for:

- Travel warnings

- Country description

- Entry requirements

- Type of government

- Safety record

- Crime rates

- Aviation safety

- Traffic safety and road conditions

- Customs regulations

- Criminal penalties

- Consular access

- Currency

- Photography restrictions

- Telephone service

- Medical facilities

If you travel frequently, this is the site you need to keep in your favorites.

The address is www.travel.state.gov.

Canadian equivalent: www.voyage.qc.ca

> *When traveling near or in a country in conflict, register with your embassy and let them know where to reach you in case of emergency or evacuation advisories.*

Because of the turmoil characterizing many parts of the world, you need to seek pertinent, adequate and above all, updated information on the country visited. Just think of the medical status of China and Canada that was changing weekly during the SARS epidemic. In addition to the general information, don't hesitate to ask about security measures and personal protection in the place you visit. Proximity to great restaurants and shops are not important in the present era. Here is a checklist of questions you should ask before leaving the country:

- Does your hotel have a shuttle bus or taxi fleet? If so, use it!

- How old is the hotel and does it have modern fire protection (sprinklers)?

- Do not choose a hotel close to a United States consulate/embassy or a close ally of the U.S. When terrorists set a car bomb at the British Consulate in Istanbul in November 2003, it destroyed part of the neighboring hotel.

- Is there more than one door lock in your room? Security guards patrolling the area? Access to your room by a balcony? Ask for a room below the 7th floor, because that is as far as a fire truck aerial ladder will go, in a modern country.

- Do you have easy access to telecommunications? Internet? Phone, fax, for example?

- Get the phone number of the nearest embassy or consulate, along with the address and working hours.

- Verify with your insurance company for which items you are covered; never assume you are automatically covered.

- Are there medical facilities nearby?

- Does your bank have a branch or affiliate in that particular city?

When contacting the local consulate:

- Inform them of the purpose of your trip. Ask if you need any papers other than a passport to get into the country.

- Ask if there are any civil restrictions such as the use of a camera, prohibited areas, curfews, alcohol consumption, etc... If there are any, they will let you know.

> *If you travel extensively, have a copy of your prescription eyeglasses with your office or a relative. That way, you can get it faxed to you if you break or lose your glasses.*

- If you are taking prescribed drugs, confirm legality and quantities you are allowed to carry. Some countries (especially in the Middle East) can require a letter from your doctor if you carry certain narcotics and painkillers. Always carry them in their original containers.

- If you are bringing anything other than your normal traveling accessories and clothes, verify with the consulate if you are allowed to enter the country with animals, firearms, alcohol, food, plants, artifacts, etc... For instance, you could be fined and go to jail if you enter Canada with a garment or article from an endangered species such as ivory bracelets and sculptures, products from marine turtles, skins, teeth and claws from felines.

PACKING YOUR LUGGAGE

What you bring with you could either get you into trouble or get you out of difficulty.

Legal documents

Many trips turn into disasters because of a stolen or lost passport. Here are a few tips to get you out of trouble quickly. Make three copies of your passport (only the page with the photograph and the number) and put a copy in your carry-on

> *Never put your valuables in your checked luggage. The same rule applies to passports, plane tickets and medication.*

bag, another one in your check-in luggage and leave a third one with a family member or your employer. A copy does not replace an original but it will greatly accelerate your identification and the replacement by your country's Embassy.

Important note: Put your passport in a cover to conceal your citizenship; nobody needs to know where you are from when waiting in line at immigration. If you travel in a region in conflict or at war, **do not carry a passport stamped by an enemy country**. For instance, it is not wise to travel to certain Arab countries with several Israel stamps in your passport, and vice-versa. If that is the case, get a new passport before you leave. For some countries, it is possible to get a stamped visa on a separate sheet, without any markings on your passport. A good travel agency will supply you that information. And again a reminder: get the phone number of the closest Embassy before you leave, should you travel to an unfamiliar country.

You may want to make copies of your plane ticket, traveler's checks, along with addresses and phone numbers of your hotel and contacts abroad. A good travel agency will make it part of their service and they should do it automatically. If they don't, then ask for it! Leave these copies with your office or a relative.

Be advised that an airline is not obliged to replace a lost plane ticket, and if they do, it will be at significant cost to you. It is a misconception to think that your name is in the computer and all there is to do is to identify you. They may ask you to purchase a new ticket at full price or pay a penalty. Whenever possible, travel with an electronic ticket, you can copy them and they are easy to retrieve when lost.

Make sure that your will and your insurance policies are in order and active. Again, make several copies of the emergency number for your medical coverage or write that number in many places.

When buying pre-flight insurance, make sure medical evacuation is covered in case of illness or accident.

What you should leave behind when packing your suitcase:

During a seminar in which corporations from several countries were attending, a British executive who did business in Bogota casually put his briefcase on the table to get something out of it and what I saw attached to it qualified him as a prime target for kidnappers. What a better way to show your status than to hang on the handle a V.I.P. gold card pass supplied by an airline to access private airport lounges. Of course, I took the opportunity to bring the point across about appearance and mannerism. Remember, average people are not interesting targets for criminals seeking ransom money.

- Any family souvenirs that have any monetary value.

- Any excess credit cards; you don't need to bring your three gas cards on top of your regular cards. Bring two cards and separate them, one in your wallet and hide another one in your carry-on luggage or money belt, in case you get robbed.

- War veteran or army reserve identification, or anything that can link you to the police or the military. You will see later on how it can get you into serious danger.

- Any literature or magazine politically sensitive or containing nudity.

- Flashy jewelry, expensive watches and the designer luggage for which you paid a fortune. Use it for weekend getaways by car. Humble accessories do not attract criminals.

- Items and materials considered dangerous by the FAA such as: matches, lighters, lighter fuel, fireworks, any pointy metal objects, such as nail files, scissors, screwdrivers for eyeglasses, etc... If prosecuted, the law provides for a fine of up to $27,500 and up to five years in prison. In case you are not sure, you can see the list and get detailed information by consulting the FAA web page at
    http://www.faa.gov/passengers/Baggage.cfm

What you should bring:

- Do not bring clothes that project an image of wealth. If you have to bring a business suit, don't wear it when traveling. Only use it when you get to your destination, for a particular event or purpose.

> *Put an eye-catching feature on your suitcase for easy identification. It is also wise to leave an address inside your luggage in case the outside tag gets ripped off.*

- According to federal statistics, two thirds of plane crash victims die from extensive burns after the aircraft has hit the ground. The FAA (Federal Aviation Administration) suggests this:

  - Wear natural fiber clothing such as cotton, wool or denim because synthetic material will dissolve when heated.

  - Cover your body as much as possible but wear loose clothing.

> *Don't put young children in an aisle seat. They tend to grab things and their arms could get hurt if bumped by a service cart or a person.*

- Wear flat heel shoes when you take the plane; it is safer in case of emergencies and also much more comfortable.

- Always bring a small bottle of water because you dehydrate faster in a plane. Also, if you are involved in an emergency landing, you can wet a piece of cloth or handkerchief to protect you from inhaling smoke. It is wise to be prepared for this because statistics show the majority of plane crash victims do not die from an impact but from toxic fume inhalation and from being burned.

- Bring an extra pair of eyeglasses or contact lenses.

- If you are going to a region of the world in conflict or at war, verify the possibility of bringing your cell phone or renting one upon arrival.

- Do not wrap gifts you bring with you. You could be asked to open them at the security checkpoint.

SPECIAL PRECAUTIONS
FOR EXECUTIVES

Traveling executives are a target for assassinations and kidnapping by many terrorist groups, especially in third world countries. The Oklahoma City National Memorial Institute for the Prevention of Terrorism reports close to 4,000 fatalities caused by terrorist incidents on businesses only, from 1997 to the end of 2003. It is interesting to observe that the phenomenon existed before 2001 because approximately half of the fatalities occurred between 1997 and 2001, when many corporations had little concern about this problem.

GRAPHICAL SUMMARY

Selected Target:

Business

Selected Time Frame:

**01/01/1997
to 04/21/2004**

Total
Incidents:1118

Total
Fatalities:3893

Total
Injuries:2974

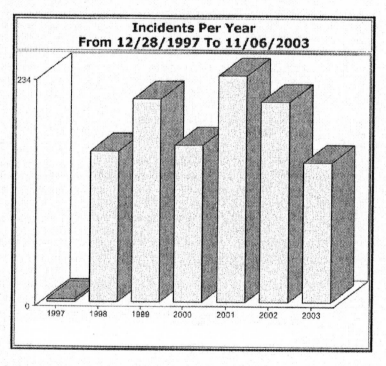

Source: RAND-MIPT terrorism incident database

If your company is involved directly or indirectly with the military industry, you are at great risk if you are identified by the wrong people. Here are some rules to observe that may save you from serious trouble:

- When traveling from one country to another, avoid carrying information that can link you to your company. Never use your business card as an I.D. tag on your luggage, or anything with a company logo on it. Check in anything that connects you to your company. You can't do serious work on a plane anyway. That's right, just relax and enjoy the movie or read a book.

> *Facilitate the screening process by taking your coat off ahead of time and having your ticket and I.D. within easy reach. Don't wear shoes that are difficult to remove.*

- Do not publicize your itinerary. Only your family, your executive assistant and travel agent should know your whereabouts.

- Never wear corporate jewelry when traveling or any expensive personal jewelry.

- Bring credit cards identified with your name only, without reference to your company.

- Replace your passport if it shows extensive traveling because it will draw attention to you if you are taken hostage.

- Don't dress like a businessperson. You are less likely to attract attention if you dress casually or dress like the local people.

- Follow the advice in the first chapter about copying legal documents and get detailed information about your hotel and the location of the Embassy closest to your hotel or place of residence.

- Try to travel with an airline from a neutral country.

- Never confide to anyone on the plane about what you do or the purpose of your trip. That information could cause you problems at a later time.

- When choosing a hotel, the opinions of the experts are split on that issue: the average hotel makes you more anonymous but the upscale luxury hotels are more secure. I go for the more secure option.

- Never reveal the purpose of your trip, nor your company name to the hotel counter. Just give your name, address, credit card number and departing date.

> *Once you locate your seat in an airplane, always count the rows between you and the nearest front and rear exits. You will be able to find your way out with your eyes closed, should you have to leave a plane filled with smoke.*

- If you must rent a car, don't rent the luxury models. Rent a car that is most common in the area you are visiting. Do not reveal you are a foreigner by leaving maps or traveling bags on the seats. Store your bags in the trunk and the maps in the glove compartment.

- Never carry bank statements with you; it may reveal wealth and a simple mugging can turn into a kidnapping.

- If you cannot buy a phone calling card, always carry local coins when you leave your hotel. They will come in handy if you need to use a public payphone for an emergency. Have someone from the hotel show you how to use a payphone and make sure you have with you at all times the numbers for the police, your hotel and the embassy. Bring enough coins for two or three calls.

- If you are picked up at the airport by someone that doesn't know you, under no circumstances should that person hold a sign with either your name or company name. This is a very dangerous practice in a Third World country where kidnappings are becoming epidemic. Use a code instead, e.g. red hat, or umbrella, etc.

Countering kidnappings

You don't have to be a celebrity executive to be a target of kidnappers. Hundreds of executives are kidnapped every year and the trend is on the rise.

You are always most vulnerable when you leave your hotel. If someone or a group is plotting to steal or kidnap you, they will make careful observations of your movements around the hotel and choose the right moment to make their move. Your greatest risk is when you leave your hotel. You can reduce your risk significantly by taking these steps:

When taking public transportation, put your fare money in a separate pocket from your wallet. Experience has shown that pickpockets will observe exactly where people put their wallet, and follow their victims in a crowd to steal from them.

- Always try to leave your room and hotel at ir-regular hours. This way, it is more difficult for aggressors to establish a pattern and you may discourage them to a point where they will want to find an easier target.

- If your hotel has more than one entrance/exit, use it at random.

> *When taking the subway, always stick with the crowded cars. Predators always look for people by themselves in empty cars.*

- Always notice who is at the door when you enter or leave the hotel.

- Never hesitate to take a taxi, even when you have a short distance to walk, but remember, do not let the taxi choose you!

- If you have to walk, choose well-illuminated streets, don't take shortcuts, and stay on main ar-teries. When walking, do not look hesitant, even if you are lost. Maintain a well determined pace to show you are familiar with the area and know where you are going.

- In restaurants, don't choose a table close to side-walks or windows. Sit in a place so as to have a good view of the entrance.

How to get into your car
in a parking lot or a public garage
if in a high-risk environment:

- Be vigilant; look around you, have your key ready, look into the car and between the seats.

- If you are parked next to a van, enter your car from the passenger door or get escorted by police or security. Many kidnappers or serial killers attack their victims by pulling them into their van when the victim is attempting to get into his/her car.

- You should do the same if one or more males are sitting in a car parked next to you. Don't get in, wait till they leave or get assistance. It's better to be paranoid than dead!

Kidnap and ransom insurance

K and R insurance can cover both personal and corporate assets. It can include all or some of the following: ransom payment, loss of income, property extortion, travel expenses for the victim's family, interest on bank loans, medical and psychiatric care.

For fear of increasing the risk to the person insured, coverage must be kept secret. Should a client brag about it, his claim would be denied if discovered. Individuals covered are often unaware of the insurance.

Some companies can give you up to $100 million in coverage. Demands are often around $10 million and average ransom payments are on the rise. Kidnappers do not usually get the amount they initially request. It is generally settled around 20 percent of the demand. Statistics show an average death rate of nine percent for all kidnappings. These numbers are much higher in the Soviet Union where the Mafia is reluctant to negotiate and extremely brutal.

Many kidnappings occur in a taxi. If you are going to use taxis on a regular basis during your stay in a high crime city, get your hotel to introduce you to a few drivers they know are safe and make arrangements with them in order to reduce your risk. Random kidnappings are also done at knifepoint or gunpoint. They take the victim to an ATM machine to empty his/her bank account and then release them the same day.

According to the annual Hiscox survey, the countries most at risk are in order: Columbia, Mexico and Brazil. Eastern Europe and some parts of Asia are becoming a higher risk. Many companies are not aware of this situation. If you are an executive working in a foreign country, you should inquire about your risk of being kidnapped.

One big advantage to purchasing K and R insurance is that a threat assessment is done and preventative measures can be taken. These firms usually have the best security consultants in the business.

Here is a list of the major K and R insurance companies:

- Hiscox Ltd.

- Black Fox International Inc.

- Chubb Insurance Company of Canada

- Lloyd's of London

AIRPORTS
AND TRAIN STATIONS
ARE HAZARDOUS PLACES

Terrorist organizations are obsessed with the aviation industry and an airport is one of the most dangerous places to be when you travel. It is a choice target because of the huge turmoil it causes and the visibility it gets. It is not a place to linger. It's easy to find a crowd at almost any time of day and security is practically non-existent, unless you have passed the security checkpoint. There are no security checks done for firearms or explosives on anyone entering the airport building. For example, a citizen of Venezuela was arrested on February 13, 2003 in London's Gatwick airport after authorities found a live grenade in his luggage. He had flown on a British Airways flight from Caracas before the device was found. Fortunately, no one was hurt but this kind of incident should trigger more severe measures in all public airports. Many attacks have been perpetrated in front of airline counters in the past because of this lack of control, and the danger remains because nothing is being done about it.

It should be absolutely essential to perform searches at the entrance of the airport property, as was the case after a bomb killed 5 and injured 26 people on September 14, 1986 at Kimpo Airport (Seoul) South Korea. I happened to be there one week after the incident and I must say the authorities did quite a good job to prevent any type of future incident. Amongst additional security measures that were implemented, metal detectors were installed at the entrance of the building and vehicles entering the premises were randomly searched. What I find unfortunate is that some of these measures were only put in force temporarily.

Do your shopping only in the secured area of the airport. If you drive someone, just drop him or her off. You don't need to escort them to their gate, at least not until security is improved.

- When it comes time to make your seat selection, choose a window seat near the emergency exit. Your second choice is always a window seat, avoiding first and business class. Terrorists usually set up their quarters in the front of the plane. They tend to brutalize or kill passengers that project wealth, are connected to the military industry or simply because they are more visible. We will elaborate on that subject later on in this guide. As a rule of thumb, pick a window seat in coach class.

- Call the airline in advance to confirm departure time to avoid spending too much time at the airport.

- Avoid standing in a crowded waiting line to check in. The safest way to go through an airport is to arrive when most of the waiting line has gone through. There is a history of attacks at

> *Where available, use the plastic shrink wrap service at airports. Not only will it protect your bags, but it prevents tampering.*

crowded airline counters serving airlines from the U.S. and Israel. The most memorable cases happened in Rome and Vienna in 1985 and Los Angeles in 2002. In each of these cases, attackers opened fire on the waiting line and in one case a grenade was thrown.

- If you are worried about missing your flight, arrive first at the counter and go through the security zone immediately.

- The safest place to be is on the other side of the security checkpoint. If you need to eat or shop,

do it there. If the airport does not provide a secure area for passengers, then stay away from
crowds.

- Be alert at all times and identify emergency exits as you pass by.

- If you see or hear any commotion, get out of the
area. There are usually enough guards in the airport to look after things.

- Be alert to set-ups and distractions organized
by pickpockets and thieves. It could be a child
that spills something on you, or an adult that
finds a non-existent stain on your clothes.
Next thing you know, your handbag is gone!
This applies to any crowded place like the
subway or a train station.

> *When traveling with young children, take all essential items in a carry-on bag. Flight delays and lost baggage can prevent you from giving proper care i.e.: food, medication, diapers, etc...*

- When arriving at your destination, stay with
your luggage until you see it being placed in the
taxi or shuttle bus.

- Choose a well identified taxi line, and don't let

someone direct you to a cab, unless he or she is an identified airport official.

- Explosives seem to be a preferred method for many terrorist groups. More than 5,000 incidents are reported for a six-year period according to the RAND-MIPT terrorism database system. Never sit next to a garbage bin, a box, parcel or unattended baggage, or a vending machine. They are potential places to hide explosives. Don't sit facing big plated glass; sit next to support columns. It is the safest place in case of detonation.

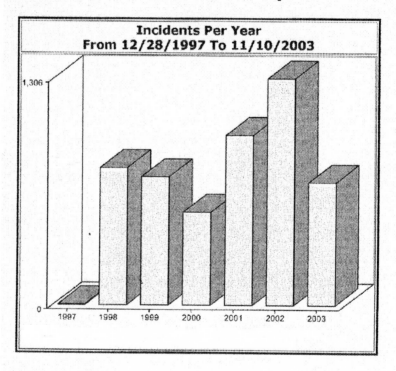

Source: RAND-MIPT terrorism incident database

It is not easy to protect yourself from an imminent explosion but there is something you can do. Here is an excerpt from "Self-help Handbook to Combating Terrorism", JS Guide 5260, produced by the Office of the Joint Chief of Staff, July 1996 for U.S. service members traveling aboard.

Actions if attacked

- "Dive for cover. Do not run. Running increases the probability of shrapnel hitting vital organs or the head.

- If you move, belly crawl or roll. Stay low to the ground, using available cover.

> *Two things flight attendants won't tell you during an emergency landing:*
> 1. *Wet a piece of cloth to put in your mouth and protect you against smoke.*
> 2. *When the plane stops, don't wait for instructions, just get out!*

- If you see grenades, lie flat on the floor, feet and knees tightly together with soles toward the grenade. In this position, your shoes, feet and legs protect the rest of your body. Shrapnel will rise in a cone from the point of detonation, passing over your body.

- Place arms and elbows next to your ribcage to

protect your lungs, heart and chest. Cover your ears and head with your hands to protect neck, arteries and skull.

- Responding security personnel will not be able to distinguish you from attackers. Do not assist them in any way. Lie still until told to get up."

Rail Passengers

The train attacks in Madrid on March 11, 2004 were a serious demotivator for railway travelers around the world. Even though passenger trains have historically been the safest means of transport, those events have highlighted how vulnerable the train system is. Security measures are far behind that of the aviation industry and improvements are required to restore travelers' confidence.

It is very difficult to ensure adequate protection on account of the magnitude of territory covered by thousands of miles of tracks subjected to all forms of sabotage. In fact, one week after the Madrid attack, a bomb was recovered on a track near London, fortunately before it could do any harm.

You need to intensify your alertness when going through a train station because these areas are generally poorly protected and always crowded. Train stations are located in the downtown area in most cities and they attract more unwanted people than airports located on the outskirts.

- When in a train station, spend as little time as possible in the public areas and stay away from crowds as much as possible.

- Do everything possible not to show you are a stranger, otherwise you will attract swindlers and criminals. If you pay for your tickets in cash, use the local currency to reduce your chances of being noticed.

- Apply the same principles as mentioned in the previous chapter, i.e.: always locate emergency exits as you move around in the station and conceive your plan on how you will get out once in your seat.

- Keep your passport and money hidden close to you. Train stations are very lucrative places for pickpockets and criminals. In certain countries, they work as a team and snatch purses off people. By the time you look back to see what hit you, they are gone through the crowd.

- Stay away from garbage bins, vending machines and any unattended luggage or packages, whether you are in the station or the train car. The risk is so high that in the United Kingdom, garbage bins have been removed from all train stations.

- Unless you are with a group, don't choose an empty car. If you have to, move to another car as the train drops people on the way.

IS YOUR HOTEL SAFE?

Hotels are hard to secure because of the multiple passageways, entrances and public areas. The industry is slow to make changes because of the costs involved. Just read the following and come to your own conclusions:

"After the Bali bombing, the trade publication *Hotel Asia Pacific* surveyed more than 300 international hotels (almost 60 percent of respondents were in the Asia Pacific Region) and found that one in three hoteliers had concerns about safety on their properties. But 60 percent had not increased their security budgets."

At the time, the magazine's editor and survey organizer, Steve Shellum, called the lack of action "not just scary, but an indictment on the industry". (*USA Today*, March 28, 2003)

Criminals know that hotels are difficult to secure and that little is done about it. It doesn't matter which country you are in; you can reduce your risk of being a victim by following these simple rules:

- First, use the bellboy and get a receipt immediately for every piece of luggage.

- When checking in, do the same as checking into an airline, have your carry-on in front of you and your luggage leaning on your leg.

- Try to get a room between the second floor and the seventh floor, as mentioned earlier. You also need to avoid the first floor because of easy access to your window or balcony. You need also to avoid rooms in the front or with a view on a parking lot. Car bombs are often left in front of the hotel or in an adjacent parking lot.

> *If you don't speak the language, have a hotel staffer write you an emergency note to carry with you. Have one to signal the police, one for a doctor or hospital or one for the nearest phone.*

- Familiarize yourself with the emergency exits. You normally find evacuation plans close to elevators (Now there's something to do when waiting for your elevator!). Count the doors from your room to the emergency exit. If there is smoke, you will have to crawl.

- Go to your room accompanied by the bellboy and have him open the room and turn on lights to ensure the room is vacant. This is a habit that I picked up since I once entered a room wrongly assigned to me. Fortunately for me, the occupants were out. You should do it for safety reasons and also to avoid any embarrassment in case there are people in the room when you enter it. Just let the bellboy deal with it!

- Check all windows and doors for locks.

- Use the peephole each time someone knocks on your door and verify with the reception if someone says he or she is a hotel employee, unless you have called room service.

- When staying in your room, use all the locks at your disposal, even in daytime.

- Use the hotel security box for valuables; however, your passport should be with you at all times.

- Never leave your key with the clerks at the front desk, nor notify them that you will be away for a period of time. Two representatives of my former employer had left their keys at the front desk, saying they would be back from dinner in about two hours. Upon their return, all their belongings

> *Always travel with a small flashlight and leave it on your bedside table at night for emergencies.*

had disappeared along with their suitcases. You shouldn't confide in anyone about your where-abouts, not even the hotel staff. Leave the impression that you are in your room most of the time by leaving your TV set switched on when absent or hanging the "Do not Disturb" sign on the outside door knob.

- When leaving your hotel, choose a well identi-fied taxi line and have the doorman find one for you. When in doubt, never let anyone force you to drive with him or her if they have chosen you.

- As mentioned previously, always carry enough coins to make two phone calls when leaving the hotel. You should have the hotel, police and embassy phone numbers with you at all times.

- Try not to look like a busy businessperson around the hotel. Just look like a low-key tour-ist; no one is interested in kidnapping a tourist.

> *When arriving at a hotel, get in the habit of taking a hotel business card. You may need it for a taxi or for an emergency call.*

If you think this is pushing it, think again. In Columbia alone, there have been more than 3,000 kidnappings over the last five years. Dur-ing those years, more executives were kidnapped or killed than politicians. This phenomenon is on the rise in many other countries such as Mexico, Brazil and in Eastern Europe.

When going out.

At the beginning of this guide, we mentioned that the political climate being what it is, (i.e. infrequent, but still-alarming terrorist bombs detonating in many countries), you should stay away from crowds, especially in airports, government buildings and demonstrations, no matter what the event. If you have to be there and you hear any commotion, don't look, don't freeze, just run away. Stay away from clubs, bars and restaurants heavily frequented by Americans. Tragically, U.S. citizens have become a prime target of religious terrorist fanatics, as well as citizens of countries allied to the U.S.

If you hear gunshots, get down immediately and face the ground. Do not stand until you are sure the danger has passed, and just wait until a few people start to get up before you do. Do not attempt to help rescuers and never pick up a weapon. If you must move, crawl on your stomach.

If you are in a region with a history of suicide attacks, read carefully this quote from "Informed Source Bulletin, April 2nd, 2003" on early signs to look for, moments before a suicide attack:

"Given the possibility for terrorist martyrdom to be stepped up against the United States and Great Brit-

ain, a couple of points to look for when in crowded places:

- *Men or women with the "wrong" (out of place) clothes for their environment*

- *Look for persons who appear to be in "silent prayer". Many homicide bombers send up last-minute silent prayers before they detonate.*

- *If you are in public and you hear "ALLAH AKBAR", don't look. Just run. They have pronounced that (their) God is great and they are on their way to heaven."*

SPECIAL SECTION
FOR WOMEN

On the morning of December 4, 2001, I was in an airport, waiting for a flight to Kansas City. Sitting on a stool in a crowded lounge, I struck up a conversation with a young woman working for a well-known electronics firm. She told me how much her job as a sales representative had changed since 9-11 and that she had to adjust to that. My immediate reaction was to assume that her traveling had been reduced drastically from what it was before September 2001. To my surprise, she said that she was traveling more than ever before, because her boss had requested she look after the clients of other sales reps who were afraid of traveling.

What bothered me about the conversation was that within about 15 minutes, she had also told me her name, where she worked, where she lived, along with

the details of her itinerary. Had we been going to the
same city, I think she would have shared a taxi with
me, which is something a woman should never do with
a stranger, especially abroad.

Giving so much information about yourself to a total stranger is a recipe for trouble regardless of the
country you are in.

In a seminar I was giving to a group of companies,
several participants, including women, asked me "Why
do you differentiate between men and women when it
comes to countering crime while traveling?" Here are
a few of the reasons:

- Women are perceived to be physically weaker
  than the average man is and less able to defend
  themselves against aggression. They are also at
  greater risk for sexual assaults. The suggestions
  we are giving you in this section should be ad-
  hered to in any hotel, in any country in the
  world. The fact that you project the image of a
  businesswoman does not reduce your risks at all
  because in the mind of an aggressor, you are
  more likely to travel by yourself than the average female tourist. Don't wear expensive
  jewelry but do wear a wedding band, a fake one
  if you are single.

*If you are a woman, don't go to the hotel
gym if there is no permanent attendant,
unless you have a Black Belt in Karate.*

- Whenever possible, always choose flights with daytime arrivals, especially if you are going to a place for the first time, it is much safer.

- The key to your safety is your ability to fool everyone into believing that you are not alone. Aggressors will prowl your hotel, sometimes with assistance from the staff, and establish your

> *If you carry a laptop or a camera, use a diaper-padded bag. Do not use fancy leather or expensive bags, use your imagination!*

profile for possible wealth, purpose and length of stay. They could be standing next to you when you are checking into the hotel and start profiling you just by hearing your conversation with the reception clerk. Not all hotels have huge lobbies that provide privacy when checking in and popular hotels usually have busy reception desks.

- Professional desk clerks will not announce your room number out loud. If they do, and you are surrounded by people who can hear it, ask for another room immediately.

- You need only to rely on yourself for your security and safety. However, knowing how the enemy works, you are now at an advantage. The key here is to make yourself undesirable and unpredictable for anyone with bad intentions. Always remember that criminals and perverts do not look like convicts.

- As much as possible when you are traveling alone, try to get a room close to the reception desk as long as there isn't any access from outside. Under no circumstances should you let anyone know you are traveling alone, whether

> *In the majority of cases, predators will choose women with long hair or ponytails they can grab to immobilize their victims. If you have long hair and travel to unfamiliar areas, choose a hairstyle that will discourage rapists from targeting you.*

in the U.S., Canada, or anywhere else in the world. The hotel staff does not need to know you are by yourself, nor does the security staff. Make believe someone is meeting you later, such as your husband or a colleague. Ask occasionally if someone has left a message or document for you at the reception.

- As much as possible, you shouldn't make the walk to your room unaccompanied. Be creative and invent excuses or have someone carry something for you. The first time you enter your room, have the bellboy go in first to turn on the lights, and show you how to lock windows and doors. Check every corner of the room before dismissing the bellboy.

- Thereafter, every time you leave your room, always leave the lights on, TV on and open the bathroom and closet doors. This way, upon your return, you can glance quickly to make sure you are alone. If you don't like hotel staff in your room, tell the hotel you will make your own bed and get some extra towels. Hang the "Do not Disturb" sign to show the room is occupied every time you leave.

- When taking the elevator, always have your key in your hand, ready to get in your room. It's not safe to search through your handbag in the middle of the corridor in front of your room. You should do the same when going to your car; at all times, have your keys ready and look inside to see if everything is normal, then get in.

- Too often, in crowded areas, I have seen women going into their purses and wallets and having to expose a wad of bills. Arrange to have a petty cash wallet to pay for taxis, doormen, newspapers, etc. If you ever get mugged, that way you can give the petty cash wallet away instead of the real one. Get a prepaid phone card instead of using your credit card in public phones. Be especially careful when standing in a crowded bus or walking up stairs or escalators. That's when pickpockets like to strike.

- If you need to ask for directions, ask women or a couple, preferably with children.

- If a car starts to follow you when you are walking on the street, turn around and walk immediately in the other direction, It's OK to run, but not in the same direction as the car.

- Get in the habit of parking your car backward to walls and always ready to go. It can save you a lot of trouble if you need to make a quick getaway.

- When driving, if someone is trying to get your attention, or if you are bumped, keep driving to the nearest gas station or a well-lighted busy area.

- Always hide your luggage in the trunk and never leave open maps for everyone to see that you are a stranger.

- Be extremely vigilant when unexpected people show up at your room because there is practically no reason for anyone to knock on your

> *Do not accept drinks*
> *from strangers you have just met.*

door without prior notice. If and when it happens, don't open the door no matter what you are being told or what you see through the peephole. If someone represents himself as a hotel employee, get the person's name and department, and verify immediately with the reception desk. You should check the same way if you get a call from hotel maintenance or any other staff that wants to enter your room. When you are talking on the phone, pretend you are being interrupted by someone else in the room. This will discourage anyone with bad intentions who thinks you are alone. If you have to order room service, always ask for an extra set of cutlery, dishes or an extra glass for your phantom guest.

- When going to bed, use all the locks on your door, including the chain lock and check the window locks (in case a maid opened the window while cleaning your room.) Do you want to sleep better and make your room even more secure? Slide a chair under the doorknob and you can always carry a door stopper in your luggage for additional protection.

> *When using an elevator, get in the habit of standing near the alarm button.*

- Finally, when you are by yourself in the hotel, avoid getting into an elevator with suspicious looking people. If someone like that does get in after you, pretend you forgot something and walk out immediately! Don't think too hard, just get out, the next elevator can't be that far away as to delay you unnecessarily.

SURVIVAL SECRETS IN HIJACKING OR HOSTAGE SITUATIONS

Accurding to the Associated Press, there was a very peculiar announcement made by the pilot of United Airlines Flight 564 on September 15, 2001. These are the instructions that were given to all passengers:

   * *"If someone or several people stand up and say they are hijacking this plane, I want you all to stand up together. Then take whatever you have available to you and throw it at them. Throw it at their faces and heads so they will have to raise their hands to protect themselves. The very best protection you have against knives are pillows and blankets. Whoever is close to these people should then try to get a blanket over their head, then they won't be able to see. Once that is done,* *get them down and keep them there. Do not let them up. I will then land the plane at the closest place and we will take care of them. After all, there are usually only a few of them and we are 200-plus strong. We will not allow them to take over this plane." Quote from Frommer's "Fly Safe, Fly Smart", Sascha Segan, Hungry Minds, 2002.*

The images of American Airlines Flight 11 and of United Airlines Flight 175 penetrating into the twin towers of the World Trade Center have created a belief in our mind that from now on, nobody can survive a hijacking. We will not discuss in this guide what should or could have been done to prevent those horrible events of September 11, 2001 from happening. World authorities have gone to great lengths and expense to increase the level of security aboard airplanes. With the tightening of passenger inspections, cockpit fortification and the hiring of undercover sky marshals, it will take a higher level of sophistication for criminals or terrorists to take over the controls of a commercial aircraft. Nobody knows what form this will take in the next terrorism acts; we can only hope that an increasing number of travelers will know how to react and possibly come out safely from future attempts.

This is why I have researched from expert sources the basic guidelines on how to prepare for a hijacking or a hostage situation. Please understand that each situation is unique, and the advice here is to help you evaluate a situation and come out alive along with others. The decision to take an offensive course of action may be justified when you perceive the situation to be totally hopeless and it will be covered in the next section.

Even though suicide terrorism remains in our minds because of its unthinkable results, there are still criminal groups who use hostages as a commodity, therefore keeping you alive is in their own interest. The advice that follows will help you draw on your inner resources, focus your mind to think clearly and prevent despair from setting in. When hijackers carry firearms, remain passive until trained personnel or sky marshals identify themselves.

The initial phase of a hijacking or a hostage situation is the most dangerous. Terrorists are extremely tense and agitated in the first 30 minutes of the incident. **Unless you are asked a question, do not talk to them or try to have eye contact with your captors.** They may feel provoked or observed. They may think you want to identify them later to the authorities. The main thing here is to make yourself invisible and not attract any attention.

The following rules will increase your survival chances in a conventional/traditional type of hijacking.

Conventional hijacking:

- Listen carefully and follow instructions. Do not offer any resistance and don't ask any questions. Do not volunteer for anything; this would only attract attention and raise suspicion. Maintain discipline to remain on the best terms with the captors.

- Be aware that all hijackers do not reveal themselves at the same time. A lone hijacker may be used to draw out security personnel for neutralization by other hijackers, so don't talk to the stranger next to you.

- Prepare yourself for possible verbal and physical abuse, lack of food, drinks and unsanitary conditions.

- If permitted, read, sleep or write to occupy your time.

- Do not complain and never ask permission to smoke or change seats. Experience has shown that hijackers often prohibit the use of the washrooms for long periods of time. Only ask for the washroom if you are really, really at your limit.

- Do not drink alcohol. You need to keep your mind sharp and also limit your need to go to the bathroom.

- If you are in the military, army, reserve or any profession relating to police work, get rid of your cards, badges or pins. You should not carry such items. If so, you will be in great danger.

- Unless absolutely necessary, do not talk to the person next to you. Your captors may not speak your language and they might assume that you are plotting something.

- Try to calm yourself by taking deep breaths that expand your belly, not your chest. Your decision-making is impaired under high stress, so make an effort to relax and keep your strength.

- If you are in a plane, try to conceive a plan with different scenarios. Notice the exits; count the number of rows to each exit in case the plane fills up with smoke.

- Discreetly wear all pieces of clothes at your disposal if you can. This will help protect you from bullets and explosions. Clear a space in front of your legs. You should duck in there in case of a rescue attempt or gunfire.

- Accept all the food you are given, even if it does not appeal to your taste. Do not worry about poisoning; if they want to kill you, they will shoot you. Try to eat everything. You need all your strength and you don't know when you'll get your next meal. Don't ask for special food. Just take what you are given.

- You can be questioned. Prepare a story in your mind if you have any items that could draw attention or connect you to your employer. You shouldn't have any problem if you have applied the suggestions about packing your luggage given at the beginning of this guide. Keep your answers short and limit yourself to the essentials. Never volunteer an opinion, and if you are asked, just say you are not for or against their cause, and that you are not knowledgeable enough to comment.

- If you are involved in a lengthy ordeal, you can try to establish a rapport with the captors, but wait until the initial tension diminishes and some kind of a routine sets in. Always avoid discussing subjects that could become confrontational such as religion and politics. Robert Young Pelton who survived a kidnapping in Columbia was interviewed by Diane Sawyer on national television in April 2004. He gave his best advice on how to come out alive from such an ordeal. In essence, he suggests relating to the captors as human beings and seeking opportunities to talk about your family and children. Try and find out more about your captors' family, this way they won't think you are just a piece of merchandise waiting to be traded. You should not resist, but try to collaborate when asked to do something. Pelton is the author of the book: "The World's Most Dangerous Places".

- If you think you can escape, you need to carefully analyze your possibilities. If an opportunity presents itself, and you decide to take it, don't hesitate, move fast and don't look back.

- Never confide in other hostages about your state of mind or your plans; someone could turn you in just to get protection or more benefits from the captors.

- Always remember that if you are taken hostage, you are a valuable commodity. Avoid despair and keep reminding yourself that it is important for your captors to keep you alive and well.

During a rescue:

- Rescuers may produce loud noises or throw smoke bombs to create a distraction.

- As mentioned earlier, if you are in a plane, you should duck as low as possible in the space in front of your legs. In any other circumstances, drop to the floor and be still. Avoid sudden moves. Wait for instructions.

- Once released, avoid derogatory comments about your captors; such remarks will only make things harder for anyone still held captive.

Suicide Hijacking

Chances are extremely remote that you will ever be caught in a hijacking and applying the advice in the previous sections will greatly improve your chances of survival. In every situation possible, you should refrain from getting involved when matters are being taken over by sky marshals or airline attendants who have received the proper training. If they need assistance, they will ask for it. On the other hand, not all airplanes are protected by sky marshals, and flight attendants may be overpowered by terrorists. If you sense a suicide hijacking, you can still make a difference even if you have no self-defense training. Remember, the crew and assisting passengers immobilized the famous shoe bomber on the American Airlines flight.

This guide is not intended to train you in self-defense. If you want to acquire those skills, sign up in a class with a professional instructor. The advice in this section will however greatly improve your survival chances.

After carefully analyzing the situation, you may want to take action against the hijackers. Killing them is not the purpose here, but neutralizing them is essential.

A high percentage of people would like to respond but they just don't know what to do. First, think about working as a team, observe how you can help flight attendants and seek assistance from other passengers. If you decide to take action, your bare hands may not be enough. Here is a list of items you can find in an airplane that can be used to protect yourself or can be put to use to neutralize an aggressor.

- A seat cushion, a briefcase, a pillow or a service tray can be used as a shield.

- If you can move around, look for the fire extinguisher. You can either spray the aggressor in the eyes or use the tank as a weapon.

- By twisting a soda or a beer can, you can split it in half and end up with a razor-sharp weapon.

- You can slide out the steel drawer from the service cart and use it as a tool to hit and immobilize an aggressor.

- Use cans or bottles from the service cart and throw them at the aggressor. Use boiling coffee if you have to.

- Use a shoe to hit or throw and recruit other passengers to do the same.

- Crush a plastic cup and use the sharp edges as a tool to poke into any sensitive part of a person. A pen or a plastic knife can also do the same.

- Flashlights hanging on the walls, next to exits, can really impair a person when used to hit them on the head.

- If you are strong enough, break an armrest with your feet and use it as a stick.

- Use a blanket to cover the aggressor's head. It will then be easier to immobilize the aggressor with some help from other passengers.

- A portable computer can also be used as a weapon or a shield.

I hope you never have to use force but knowing ahead of time that these items exist can save your life because your decision-making is greatly impaired in a high stress situation. If you already know your options by reading these lines, the quality of your actions will be greatly improved. If you do confront a hijacker with whatever means you can use, **just give it all you've got**, you may not have a second chance.

PROTECTING YOUR TRAVELING EMPLOYEES

Does your company take special precautions for protecting employees abroad?

The answer is probably no, unless it is involved in the military industry or doing work in countries in conflict. It has now become a known fact that crime and terrorism can strike in any country, regardless of being at war or not.

It can be quite surprising to see how much detail and care is taken so no one gets hurt at work when, on the other hand, as soon as you leave the premises for a business trip, you are on your own! I guess it is the same analogy as an alarm system; you only purchase one after your house has been robbed of its contents. Your company should not wait for an incident to happen before doing something.

Corporations don't need to take extraordinary measures such as hiring bodyguards or supplying satellite phones to their executives. They should however act proactively and educate their traveling employees about changing some of their habits to take into account the new realities of the world. It's in the company's interest to protect their human resources and it can be done at very little cost just by designing some simple policies.

Here is a suggested list of topics you may cover if your company decides to establish a corporate protection policy for traveling employees:

1. Appointing a security administrator

Appoint your head of security or a representative from management to administer the protection policy. This person should keep abreast of the risk situation either by consulting the web sites at the end of this guide or by hiring specialized consultants. That person should at least read this guide and be able to summarize it and adapt it to your needs.

2. Security briefings

Each person must get a security briefing with the above-designated person before they are handed their plane ticket. To make the system more efficient, regroup all traveling employees for a general briefing. When it comes time for individuals to travel, you just have to give a specific briefing regarding the country they are visiting.

3. Record keeping

The person making the travel arrangements must keep copies of travelers' checks, passports, plane tickets and hotel phone numbers. The same is true for emergency contact persons here and abroad. Someone must keep track of the employee at all times in case of an emergency evacuation. You should know the name(s) of the person(s) visited, along with their phone and fax number or email. If the employee is visiting a country experiencing instability, the company should supply a satellite phone.

4. Check list

Produce a small pamphlet with a checklist of safety tips for each traveling employee. Use your contacts living abroad to point out specific precautions for each country.

5. Credit cards

Supply credit cards under the employee's name instead of the company name.

6. Clothing

Allow your representatives to travel in leisure clothes rather than in their business suits.

7. Choice of hotels

Based on the criteria in this guide, you can make a better choice of secure hotels. You should also consider making a policy for rental cars. Always rent an ordinary looking car so as to go unnoticed.

8. Group travel

Avoid scheduling a whole group of employees from the same department in the same plane; apply the same rule to your CEO with his executives.

9. Protocol in case of a crisis

The company should know exactly what to do in case of an employee who disappears because of an earthquake, a terrorist attack or any other unforeseen situation. It is unwise to improvise when emotions are involved and you need to take quick decisions. You need to seriously reflect about your communications with the family. Who will announce to the family? Who will look after the family during the ordeal? Does this person have the training to deal with that? What is your insurance coverage in case of an emergency evacuation? Will the company pay for the expenses, should the family wish to visit the site? And finally, you need to manage your public relations, keeping in mind that you should always inform the family before making public statements.

Package bomb signs

Executives on long-term assignments are at greater risk to be targeted by terrorists or criminals because they have an address, be it a villa, an apartment or a hotel suite. Furthermore, you and your family are vulnerable to receiving booby-trapped mail.

Here are some suspicious characteristics to look for when receiving letters or packages:

- An unusual or unknown place of origin

- No return address

- An excessive amount of postage

- Abnormal or unusual size

- Wires or strings protruding from or attached to an item

- Incorrect spelling on the package label

- A different return address and postmark

- A peculiar odor (many explosives used by terrorists smell like shoe polish or almonds and they try to cover it up with perfume).

- Unusual heaviness or lightness

- Restrictive markings like "personal" or "confidential"

- Oily stains on wrapping

- When addressed to a company, it is addressed to title only or to the wrong title with name.

The above advice should be prominent in your company mailroom for any person receiving the mail. You don't have to be a terrorist target to be vigilant with packages and letters; the sender could be a frustrated employee or ex-employee. The same above procedure applies to suspected anthrax deliveries. To know more about how to deal with anthrax, you can consult the MIPT web site at

www.mipt.org/suspected_anthrax_delivery.asp .

CONCLUSION

Crime and terrorism are not about to disappear from anybody's radar screen and no one knows which form it will take in the years ahead. For most Westerners, the increase in security measures can be shocking at times. Who would have thought we would have to remove our shoes to clear security at an airport, or have a nail file confiscated for fear it could harm someone in an airplane?

Because of this new reality, you need to acquire new habits in your daily lives and this guide is intended to do just that. You will have to create a new routine for yourself every time you plan a trip. If the homework about the country you are visiting is too much of a burden, get help from a family member; they should be more than glad to contribute to your safe return. You can also share some of the tips with your travel agency and involve them when it comes time to duplicate some of the paperwork they provide to you, along with checking hotels from a security point of view. By putting in place new safety habits, your family will be grateful to see that you are going the extra mile to ensure you return to them safely. It is just one more area of your life where you need to take more precautions.

Following the Madrid attacks in March of 2004, authorities in Europe have been innovative in their security campaigns. Signs in airports and train stations are encouraging travelers to get involved in preventing crime. For instance, one of the signs says: "If you see something, say something". They are referring to unattended luggage bags, suspicious behavior, etc... By increasing our alertness and vigilance, we can all play an important role in preventing terrorism.

USEFUL WEB SITES FOR FREQUENT TRAVELERS

1. Department of Homeland Security :
www.dhs.gov/dhspublic

Contains updated information on threat advisory and current top stories relating to national security in the U.S.A with latest press releases from the department. Shows detailed information on emergencies and disasters and many topics related to civil protection.

2. Federal Aviation Administration :
www1.faa.gov

Useful information on current airport status and frequently requested information by travelers such as baggage requirements, flying with pets, security issues and much more.

3. State Department counter-terrorism office travel warnings:
http://travel.state.gov/travel_warnings.html

The most complete source of information relating to travel warnings around the world. Specific information about each country and a list of all government resources for travelers from information on how to convert the Euros to international adoption.

4. FBI counter-terrorism website:
www.fbi.gov/terrorinfo/terrorism.htm

General information on terrorism warning and counterterrorism activities. Tip line for most wanted terrorists with some links about U.S. policy on terrorism.

5. You don't have to take it anymore:
http://www.passengerrights.com/pages/index.asp

Advice on how to make complaints and be heard. Hundreds of organizations to whom you wish to make an electronic complaint. You can get basic information about your rights as a traveler. There is even a section to read other people's horror stories.

6. Executive protection
www.pfisolutions.com

Corporate protection for multinational companies operating in high-risk countries.

7. Department of Foreign Affairs Canada, traveler assistance:
www.dfait-maeci.gc.ca

Bilingual site with travel advisories. Complete information for Canadian travelers including updates on terrorism threat. Links to other governments departments.

8. British Foreign Office:.
www.fco.gov.uk

Contains basically the same information as the above site for British subjects. The section on terrorism warning is very complete and easy to consult.

9. Phone rentals :
http://rentcell.com

Rent a cell phone in more than 130 countries. Also satellite phones you can use almost anywhere on the planet

10. General travelers resource
www.world-travel-net.com

A very diversified site with hundreds of links, travel news, tips, time zones, etc…

11. Travel tips
www.fodors.com/traveltips/

Hundreds of travel tips to make your trip a breeze and links to many travel related websites.

12. Canadian Passport Office
www.passport.gc.ca/travel_tips/trip_planning_e.asp

Tips on how to plan a trip, traveling with children and all necessary travel documents to carry abroad.

13. World weather
www.theweathernetwork.com

Weather forecast for traveling, skiing, golfing, etc... contains satellite and radar maps.

14. Airplane seat lay-outs
www.about.com

Picking your seat depending on the aircraft model.

15. Frequent business traveler
www.btonline.com

International travel news.

16. Overseas Security advisory council
www.ds-osac.org

Security exchange information between government and private sector. Very useful for companies operating abroad.

BIBLIOGRAPHY

Donald R. Kincaid, "International Conference on aviation Safety and Security in the 21st Century", Arson and explosive division, Bureau of Alcohol, Tobacco and Firearms, January 14, 1997.

Jane F. Garney, "FAA's Fly Smart Guide", FAA Administrator, September 18, 2001

"Patterns of Global Terrorism: 1999, the Year in Review", State Department report, October 4, 2001

Jerome Glazelusok, "Security Awareness for the Executive Traveler", Informed Source, March / April 1997

J. Hill, "Courses That Teach Tactics to foil Hijackers", article in the Globe and Mail, November 19, 2001.

Sasha Segan, "Fly safe, Fly smart", Hungry minds Inc. 2002

Don McKinnon, "Safe Air Travel Companion", McGraw Hill, 2002

Christopher P.P. Barnes, "The Personal Travel Safety Manual", Tally Ho Consulting, 2003

Printed in the United States
59688LVS00007B/214-216